AF338270

The Long Journey Out

The Long Journey Out

Ronald Okuaki Lieber

RESOURCE *Publications* · Eugene, Oregon

THE LONG JOURNEY OUT

Resource Publications
An Imprint of Wipf and Stock Publishers
199 W. 8th Ave., Suite 3
Eugene, OR 97401

www.wipfandstock.com

PAPERBACK ISBN: 978-1-6667-6867-1
HARDCOVER ISBN: 978-1-6667-6868-8
EBOOK ISBN: 978-1-6667-6869-5

01/08/24

For Mara & Max
My Children

Contents

Acknowledgements

"New Suffolk" *Passages North*

"The Look of Things" *The Tishman Review*

"Narcissism of Consciousness" *The American Poetry Review*

"Crete: August" *The Nation*

"Gare Montparnasse: The Melancholy of Departure" *The Seneca Review*

"Soft" *Sky Island Journal*

"Autumn Song" *The Santa Barbara Review*

"Still" *Bang!* Featured poet of the month, published as "A Lover"

"The Exaltation" *The New Ohio Review*

"Pardon Me" "Perhaps"; *Bang!* Featured poet of the month

"A Thought Problem" *The Colorado Review*

"Across" *The Poeming Piegon,*

"The Holy Ghost" *The Green Mountain Review*

"Sentiment for an Old Notion" *The New England Review*

And I have felt
A presence that disturbs me with the joy
Of elevated thoughts; a sense sublime
Of something far more deeply interfused,
Whose dwelling is the light of setting suns,
And the round ocean and the living air,
And the blue sky, and in the mind of man:
A motion and a spirit, that impels
All thinking things, all objects of all thought,
And rolls through all things.

William Wordsworth

"Lines Composed a Few Miles above Tintern Abbey, On Revisiting
the Banks of the Wye during a Tour. July 13, 1798"

Setting

Second Sunday in Ordinary Time:
After Wallace Stevens and Dr Seuss[1]

Gulls, midtide, noon. One could say,
one could surely say, it was by a sea,
a large irrthymical sea

and weather. But beach
that blue uncast January day was visited
by what, one may say, cannot be said.

Forget the long wooden pier and hot dog stand,
the taffy and candy shops
though they too were unimpeachably there

along with a few hatless woolen souls
who wandered bundled by the continental edge
absorbed in that sponge of a constant sea

and weather. One could say,
if one did care, a wind too
was blowing through their hair,

a wet, relentless, monadic wind
easterly from the sea
that made them cold and wish for home.

What brought them so unprepared
to this scape? The romantic sea,
the stormy sea, the melancholy sea

of Arnold far beyond its burden
of umbrellas, suntan
lotions and beer. Who could say?

       *

Take the lady in a room alone for the day,
an asymmetrical shape shadowed behind terrace doors.
She looked out. She saw

the gentle scrubbing of the sea
massage the rustic wooden pier, saw a gull
extend its wings and remembered a child

of another age in another day, a summer
complacency. They would fish from that pier
with mushy shrimp and squiggly bait

when father was a daddy, two tourists
in this bustling town of corn dogs and resort
hotels. Everyone

was a tourist and did touristy things—
took sun by day and slept the short nights in gritty beds.
She shared a bed with dad, so economical was

he, daddy and the child, a cumbersome
innocent couple in that batty resort town. That
passed years before now

when most the day she stood pensive
by the window, the big sliding plexiglass door window,
protected from the crucial elements.

Never did the memory go away
and never did the vista: a sky,
the watery expanse and beach

mostly empty except for a few
who wandered with downcast stare
by the strange indivisible sea, and weather.
                *

The couple with their Labrador tracking the edge
of the sea's loquacious reach—it was a game,
whose feet first wets, loses—

do not talk. Arm in arm in silence
they walk, a common silence
of separate thought. This was their day

by the sea, away from duties and impending
responsibilities, away from the perpendicular going ons
of an appointed world, a day to be alone with one another,

a day to relax. But seven years had elapsed,
seven years of companionship. She loved him, yes,
but had known of few others, and he of she,

well, there was the water. One could say
love or say acquaintances
who together that day strolled and smelled the sea,

a lively sea full of pungent fish and scaly things,
and of smells unknown. They admired
the bleached remains of an arthropod

they could not name in its open grave
no more the sea. They kicked up shells
and remarked upon her sister's anniversary.

The dog they brought, its tongue
hanging out, leaped and ran and rolled in sand
for no fence kept him confined and in.

From wooden pier
to no particular they went, the dog
a dot, the dog a bark.

One could say, they
were happy. They shared a place
and could walk together down that beach

arm in arm without any need to hear
the babble of one another's talk. Or one could say
they had little to talk about

and moved in a pattern
love left behind, a habit
hard to break of human design.

The wayward soul prostrate on the beach
saw the two with an attendant gaze
and smiled. All he saw was a red

and blue speck shimmering in a torrent
of a multitudinous sea,
and weather.

*

The gull hovering in the sky
for food—it had to fly or die—
saw the hunger satisfied

with a clam after many futile tries.
And when its belly exclaimed ok,
it perched on the pier and let out a cry.

*

The janitor in brown uniform
and company approved black rubber soled
shoes took his lunch outside

as he did the clement days
he worked. He put on his Christmas coat,
said goodbye to the receptionist.

Did she look up or was she unaware,
too busy with the telephone, or meandering
under the fluorescent glare?

He strolled the walk, the rundown
and splintered to be repaired boardwalk,
and breathed the salty frothy air.

Newspapers and gulls whipped by a wind
seemed to him portentous,
perhaps a squall rolling in.

He sat down on a bench
and collected his unfolding thought,
watched the roiling sea sketch

the increments of the tide.
How peaceful, away from the walled in rooms
where one breathed a ventilated air

and never saw the blue of sky. Here the limit
was the imaginative stretching of the eye to where
that blue met the sea, seemingly.

He ate his lunch packed by his wife: an orange,
a tuna fish sandwich, a bag of seaweed chips,
five strawberry Pocky sticks, and sipped

a ginger ale. Behind him an almost
shutdown hotel except for an open window,
a woman doing the same as he,

transfixed by the motioning sea. He too saw
some stragglers with lowered heads walk,
and someone toss

a frisbee that landed
near a fellow horizontal on the beach. How
down and out that dude must be,

mused he, to nap in such weather
and in only a shirt. But the dude got up
to return with a perfect spiral spin

the frisbee to its owner then plopped
himself to the ground again. What is he doing?
ballooned in the janitor's mind, but as soon thought

as soon demised, a grain of sand irritating his eye.
Then he attached his wandering to the incisive fact,
"Only ten minutes left till I gotta be back."
*

For the errant one on the beach
the day for him turned topsy
turvy. He laid for hours with head

propped on a pillow of sand
and observed the slow decay.
The beach, the pier, the billowy sky, all

flittered away and too the sun that burned
an opening in his eye, the eye
that could not see the gripping insistency,

each thing with a name,
each name with a "do re me"
swarming all around and in between,

between the edges and between the teeth.
Gulls, for instance, flew away
and the washing of the sea eased

into a blossoming that tamped
the simple naming of things. Things turned out
things with their "me me me" turned not

and not sprung loose and all
that whirling of a frolic sea,
birds and waves, buckets and signs,

stilled: a golden whisper,
revolving spheres, the music of friction
as things rubbed up against their vanishing.

But what came to take their place
he could never say.
What churned in his jangled mind

was the undeniable gap of time,
a before and after, a noon to dusk,
twelve to five, a dispossessed husk.

He labels it mystical and recalls
Wordsworth's sublime, then dusts himself
off, to flop back down, again.
                  *

Who could say what, for what
never left though what was no more,
not the gull nor long wooden pier.

Could one say beach
lost its sea, the sky its propensity
for blue or chartreuse?

The beach was a doll, the beach
a flower, a frayed silk
Tibetan banner commemorating

the sixtieth notion of the year,
the boardwalk a fence, the fence a hut
in a clearing, the clearing a trap,

the trap a ladder, the ladder
a pier, the long wooden pier
loyal to the sea.

One could say anything
and one says this: that
when returned

the names awaited
their pronouncement,
waited the sibilant to kiss,

the fricative to click, the b's
to burst, the t's to clatter,
the soft vowel to curl, they

awaited their hominid embrace.
The janitor puts on his coat to leave,
the fellow turns the key to his car

and a woman is eating dinner.
Beach was a beach after all, and not a fall,
beach was where the couple put their feet

one in front of the other
and walked, alone, that solitary day
by the irrhythmical sea, and weather.

The Way Across

Between

The Virginia of Highway 29,
through Bull Run and Culpepper,
over the Rappahanock and Rapidan
Rivers, past Rochelle and Schuyler—
"yall cum back an 'ave a goo' one"—
is, in deep August, tawny turned to an
almost blonde. What cultivation

stayed is renegade from a stingy
land rampant to reclaim what the local
seized as their own. Wherever the forest
yields, corn grows, or beans. Small
clumps of dung-colored trees tired
from the heat root in pastures where a bull
lows in the lull of an eroding gully.

A barn, patinaed to a rust in places golden,
stands solitary and seemingly
deserted, its roof falling in
like an old man's mouth. A simple white wooden
frame house, no shade trees, with a scruffy
bald lawn and a dirt road snaking up to its
two stories and pitched roof, crowns

it all—a stark and stubborn nobility
fiercely wedded to its responsibility
till death do they part. Out back a shed
sags with the years' weight, and tucked
in a corner near the barbed wire
fence sits the slow attrition of a Ford tractor
no more useful, overwhelmed by tall dead

weeds. The day is fast setting. The sun
spindly through the loblolly pine
plays a woman's shadow as if a marionette.
Girdled in gingham, her hair pulled to a bun,
she gathers the rows of clothes
set out to dry a few hours ago
while her three boys and girl yammer and fret

and more, tug on her blouse for attention.
With fond reprisals she shoos them away
and finishes the laundry. Inside her husband
beat from fieldwork never enough done
slumps like a question mark in his sofa
chair awaiting dinner, announced
in a once fine English stretched to a drawl

by the languor of the land. With a wave
of a hand the family is drawn round the table.
Nightfall. Doors are locked, shades closed shut.
Now and then the otherwise silence
is blasted by a barking like buckshot,
triggered by headlights crisscrossing Ruckersville
Junction. In one is a man tired from twelve

hours alone with himself. He wants to stop,
to lay his head snug in a pillow and sleep,
but he can't. He adjusts the rearview mirror
and glimpses there a beacon of light click off,
then a house vanish into a darkness everywhere
behind. And in that moment that doesn't last
long, his fatigue breaks; he imagines a home.

New Suffolk

Tomatoes ripe on the vine, heavy
with succulence, red and ready—
and the sweet corn sweetest,
fresh picked, eaten raw—the lettuce
crisp and deepened to sunset—August,
the nights lengthening toward
fall.

***

A gaggle of adolescent girls
too young to know their allure
giggle when I bicycle by. Ahead
on the corner of Sixth and Harbor Lane,
boys await, their baseball hats
set backwards, Coca Cola in hand.

***

Hair the color of
    harvested fields,
          of corn silk and dust,
hair like midnight.

***

For five days the rains fell,
torrent and drizzle, everything damp
from potato chips and books to underwear,
and on the third I watched a swallow,

drenched from the downpour, meticulously
construct a nest in the eave
of Fagin's General Store.

***

Just after the sun sets
the sky lightens and a hush
settles over the Long Island Sound.
Only then is the grief quieted
and welcomed as a long close friend
who after many years returns. Later
over a bottle of Merlot
and a plate of Calamata olives
we laugh, forgetting the bite inside a kiss.

***

Mid-sentence she traps
a bug in her open mouth, goes "Yuk" and spits it out.

"How fragrant and instant," this promise of food.

***

She was tall, brunette, and spoke with an accent. He was tall, dark,
and always excluded. They passed each other in the Post Office. She
wore black leggings and a yellow slicker. He looked from the bottom
up, as he once read the gods did, and saw in her eyes something he
thought familiar, something shared, but how could he know. Desire
plays cruel tricks. That night he could not sleep so took a walk by the
beach. There were no stars or moon because of cloud cover; only the
lights from Nassau Point punctuated the darkness. The air smelled of
rain and brine.

***

Riding tandem
down a country lane
cut through wetlands of grass
tall and top-heavy when the sudden
apple perfumes the air,

half-moon darkly behind
a cloud bank, bugs everywhere.
We head home, prepare a simple
dinner of fresh picked vegetables, then sit
cattycornered,

talk pooling between us.

***

Of all the body
the hands ache the most.
Every night they forage the bed,
careful not to bruise the sheets.
Of course no one's there, just
the imprint of what was and
a few strands of hair. So they withdraw.
And then something funny
happens. The hands reach out
and float, the fingers kneading
the air in random rhythm, as if remembering
the first time absence had a face.

The Look of Things

Sometimes trees, crabbed
    and central, a gnarled wildness
        like apple or iconographic oak.

Sometimes the names of flowers
    rapturous on the tongue, bee
        balm, bull thistle, Virginia

Blue bell, corn lily,
    noble particulars, over which
        dark birds, brilliant trailings.

Sometimes vermillion,
    celadon and summer green
        soon eviscerated, composted.

And often light—
    at evening celestial
        at dawn pallid, midwinter thin,

The air about to break
    over a lady and her child,
        scrambling for shelter, laughing

While far away in Ohio
    backs strain working the cows,
        behind them three steamed windows.

Narcissism of Consciousness: 1944, 1996, 2019

In a field in dry summer
in grainy black and white
is a man clutching
a five-year-old to his chest.

To his back stands a soldier,
profile of aim and stature,
who we know, because this
is a reproduction come across in

a book, will fire his Mauser,
detonating the Milky Way of
a brain. But in the moment
of the snapshot he lives,

cleaved to his daughter
for the last time. Imagine
that terrible knowledge,
and this innocence pleading

for *papa*. This time
he cannot kiss the hurt
or soothe her with a mime.
The soldier cocks

his rifle and steadies his finger.
You hold her closer,
your eyes search hers.
The shutter clicks.

Crete: August

Yesterday while walking home
the sun shadowing the backside

of cliffs that spine the island,
I thought I saw your profile

in what was a mountain.
And later, on the footpath

through the quilt-work valley, swallows
in twilight feeding frenzy and grapes

abundant where spit wouldn't hold,
I felt the presence of another—

but only air, the vapid whispering
of air between the thyme, the thistle.

Funny, for when we shared a bed
and ate from the same round table—

a telephone cable spool, remember?—
you were "taken for granted,"

regarded as just one cog
among the many geared tedium

of dailiness: work, the pecked
kisses, the homogenous dinner routines.

Yet how we needed each other.
I could tell you what pained me,

and you me, and we sometimes
were silent together, all of which conspired

to confuse.
Now in this darkness rimmed

by a moon and misty glow
that is Pitsidia braced in the concave

of the hills ahead, I long
to smell the clean sharp wine

of our lovemaking linger on my lip,
to have the cusp of your breast cupped

in my palm,
as this tarred asphalt road is hard

and hot in the swelter of days.
And if you were to return

it would be through a joyous humility
that I would do good, but being

as it is, I will prosper
through a sadness for you

who is everywhere ghosted
and nowhere to be.

Gare Montparnasse: The Melancholy of Departure

Notice the sun, absent, angled just out past
the picture frame, a further horizon, is
implied by a light, greenish in the distance
yet amber along the one and only avenue
there without inflection from the east
though it might be dusk, if not moonlight, and shadows
painted thinly, scuffled—in some places, for example
the colosseum's front lintel, almost parallel
to the ground and pregnant with an ambiguous terror
as are the buildings, not rendered
in perspective, skewed, their vanishing points numerous
and conflicting. Such precarious imperfections
attract us for we recognize ourselves
in the couple, two quick dabs of a brush,
menaced by the monumental geometry of the open
piazza, and thus reduced. No more is it
the well-ordered and logical
where the eye functioned within a hierarchy of space.
Even the colors are all wrong. Desolate
and mixed-up we have arrived at the hour
of exile from that most close to us
and so your eyes recede into an invisible
rendering of a childhood memory I cannot read.
Caught in this strange and alien place
prepared for us by our forefathers, we stand,
hosted by this brutish and eerie light,
discussing notions of antiquity exemplified
by the busts and statues sometimes dwarfing us.
I argue for the green bananas yet am drawn

by the wind raised in your hair. The wind
blows straight the festive pennants atop the building,
but there is no clamor of it rending
the quiet of this autumnal moment.
Nothing much happens. I brush aside
the tendrils from your forehead, elsewhere people
are sitting down to dinner, the market is closed.
We have that outward look of love, but as this painting
alludes to an illusion of correctness, and is just
that much off, thus unsettling, about that difference
we, too, quiver with unrest. Somehow we just don't meet.
And I want to say something, when the echo
of a train's loud whistle disturbs the silence.
Turning, we see it, locomotive and churning,
cut the horizon and it is you that remarks upon
the incongruity—the train's smoke billows
vertically, bent back neither by its insistent
forward motion nor the wind
which is now gusting in strong blasts.
The train will not stop in our small provincial village
to arrive someplace else, the same hour,
the same bad weather, while we leave one another
for separate parts of town
with something less decisive than goodbye.

Concordance

Outside the window of this barge banked against
the many layered landfill of Fort Lee, New Jersey

a grey mist shrouds the island city
now November and drizzling. Two gulls

skim the Hudson's brackish waters and a sailboat
motors downstream toward the vast tomorrows

of the sea. From out of the drift
clinging neither to water nor air

steps forward the man, Wallace Stevens, middle-aged, mid
life on his methodical way

to the Hartford Connecticut Life Insurance Building
dressed in a grey woolen pinstripe business suit.

He hears, while walking the lavender and blooms
that harbor the lane, this music:

Death is the mother of beauty,
whereupon I am standing before an alpine

picture window bathed in the afterwash of an afternoon's ease.
The broad umbrella of a sycamore shadows the front lawn,

its limbs outstretched and glistening
with moisture. On one, a drop

of rainwater curls. I turn
toward the hallway dim with the coming dusk

to join my lover running water for our bath.
I can almost hear the water splashing now

when this, too, is dredged up
from that other man, more stern,

whose thought, some say, is as supple as muscle:
And the time of death is in every moment,

an old knowledge from the Bhagavad Gita, when Krsna,
the conch shell quiet by his side, to Arjuna turns and ...

she says something I can't make out,
a clear note drowned in the bathwater's rush.

That was Verscio in May—midday showers beneath snow
peaked mountains, often invoked

for solace when sad, as if the memory
could nourish me. Yet I have missed

the verve and luster of that followed
in the wake of a summer day,

summer's past. Imagine: she and I scrubbing
each other down, while unnoticed, a blue

breasted jay darts between the green backdrop of leaves,
the droplet falling mid-air till now it is rain

and muddy waves slapping the barge where I sleep tonight,
the gulls nowhere in sight, the boat long gone.

Soft

The flush before the kiss,
Fog hovering over
The Peconic Bay, flat

Except for the short waters lapping its
Shore. The flutter
In the sumac giving up

Summer. Pollen
Sallying in air becalmed,
A spider's web billowing in a morning breeze.

The damp air,
First chill settling
In.

Autumn Song

It sweeps through
    like cloud shadow floating
        across cornfield and hillside:

A gentle leaving,
    an emptying
        the chest hollowed out—

I call the caress sadness—
    and sometimes without warning
        it swells, like yesterday in leaf-changing

Season, while hiking
    Bald Mountain, Mara,
        my ten-year-old, poked

Fallen leaves into a glistening
    cascade—white water, black rock,
        a tumble of noises, and I cross stream.

Something about her
    ten-year-old play, her lolly-
        gagging in the blush of

Early autumn light
    brisk and distinct,
        stunned me, and again

That feeling rolling
      through until distilled in
            a few tears I wiped away.

There was nothing
      to say, and I wanted to say
            something: she on one

side, me on the other
      water
            between us.

Homing

All morning the foghorn's
slurred soundings spell the known route

that to veer any closer
is to crash upon the shoals, to flounder there,

in those rocks, the shallow salt waters. What lurks
we wonder beyond that grey effluvium whose veils

lure with our passing? From what, other
than death, are we cautioned?

What was revealed, what boon,
that these bleatings warn us away

our living intact,
our dialects still with us?

Still

It was a moment, if that,
Among the many diversionary and picayune
Moments, so many in a grey day where
The bristled strokes of a neighbor sweeping the stone
Floor of the patio garden below and a hacking
Cough disturbed a calm sought for and intermittently
Found that morning, balmy,
Unusual for October, more so for the grey
From which one expected a brisk slap, not
The diaphanous embrace of air, which quickened an uease
Growing with the steady sweeping of a broom over stones,
And I remember standing, looking down into the still green garden,
Transfixed by the stark fact of ivy and brick, eave
And pigeon, and a man bent over a wooden broom, coughing,
Against a grey backdrop—and it had to have been just then,
The moment between intimation and thought—that a drift
Of silence just out of reach, beyond the dome of sky
From somewhere deep inside, somewhere ancestral, brushed
Me faintly, like a breath, all my skin alert,
Apprehensive, and in in my ear whispered
What I am only now beginning to hear.

The Exaltation

In dry season in equatorial Chad, the Sahel is so hot the soil
Chars to red dust, the grass to a blonde bristle, heat bearing down like affliction

And because the land blisters and coastal Africa is forested, humid and cool, air
Is sucked easterly, darkening the horizon with fury into which a man, tending

The village flock stares, a wave so sudden and massive the Dogon has little time
To corral the sheep before the air erupts with stinging needles. The storm

Sweeps across the continent until in the Atlantic thunderheads and wind
Marry the doldrums, and a hurricane is born. Its updraft plunges the ocean, and swells

Spiral westward across the open sea to loom large on beaches lining the American
Eastern seaboard as in Montauk Long Island where surfers

Scan the near horizon for the darkened lines their kind read. It's what they've prepared for
The summer afternoons and cool September dawns before work, that one stirring

Pitched perfect just where a surfer waits, and he paddles to catch the lip, a chthonic uprise
Heaving him high to which he surrenders, riding the rolling level underneath into rapture

That I as a ten-year-old in the thick of the Ozarks heard in the tree tops swaying
Back and forth, a thousand miles away. The shepherd, surrounded by family, stokes

The charcoal embers with dry twigs, the surfer packs his board,
And the hurricane splinters wooden homes in Kill Devil Hills. I am joined.

In Passing

1.
     Mid May in downtown
Manhattan the heat swells
In slow undulating drifts.
Relief is a virtue where each move
Is calculated, otherwise
The bananas blacken in the porcelain
Bowl, the faucet drips.
Already before the sun crests
The tarred rooftops, streets
Bloom with tank-topped
Youths wired to an irreducible
Beat and idling engines
Choke the torpor with
Caustic dioxides. On the corner
In the shade of a tenement three
Men sip 40s from brown
Paper bags, shuffle loose
Feet. They talk of horses,
Of Santo Domingo, of "la vida
Mejorado alla," and always
"Alla," over there. These are
The dog days of ripening
Too heavy for the heart's
Small hold. Morning long I
Burn for a vision, but each turning
Reveals a spool of melon rinds
And orange peels, fat clucking
Pigeons sooty in the eaves of

A crooked, unrelenting light. Those
Three will keep on keeping on
Until their shadows trip on a sidewalk
Crack and tomorrow take up
Their leanings, I will rise
To the same body in the same room,
Bruised imperceptibly by a strange
Half remembered dream, and that deaf
Dumb music will change but never that
One steady, awful beat.

2.
    Just yesterday, a sunshower
Coaxed me from a morning lull
Into a pleasing although brief repose
And I wanted more sweet
Rain but could not prod
From the sky its release. The waters
Passed by and over a swath of the north
Atlantic, like all other North's—grey,
Grievous, and raging—drenched
An ocean in need of no more
And a trawler with its crew of 17.
O but how transfigured the world
Seems then, everything keen
With a wet, translucent glaze
And the air leeched clean
Of its urban putrescence. I
Could smell again the faint
Musk of the sexual that culled
From the forgotten the fragrance
Of a southern summer night. Three
Of us read John Donne's
"The Flea" but in our stupor could
Not decipher "three sinnes in killing
Three" so we smoked ourselves silly

And headed out into a fog
Collapsed around all things. Touch
Was our seeing, the handrail
Slick and moist as we finger
Our way down the wooden stairs onto
Glimmering cobblestone streets
To arrive at the Governor's palace
Lit by a single electric arc
Lamp. We grope past the light's
Fringe, feeling the dark with
Outstretched palms when the first
Quiver surprises—the prickly fresh cut
Leaves of the Maze, cool and wet, and
I am afraid and wondrous and that
Feeling rushes through me again
And again, lost as we are
In the Maze's dead ends.

3.
    Where is the end
Among scaffolding and cranes,
Among toy stores and record
Profits, someone waking to a sour
Taste, the shades drawn, someone
Dressing for Goldman Sachs, someone
For Skansa USA. I find always
The something else and not
What I hurt for, this life
The bad end of my want.
A single arched orchid
On my windowsill
Will not stem it, an eagle slicing
The morning sky above
The Kennebeck will not
Transcend it, the warm familiar
Hand in mine will

Not assume it. Below a mother
Hums an inaudible tune to
Her newborn cradled
To her chest. The infant is
Soothed, its ear nuzzled to her
Heart and its steady thrum. But
The other ear hears a distant
Saturday, where three dogs scuffle
For scraps and vendors are stocking
Their carts, the day calm, cloudless and dear.

The Wanderer

Again, dis-
lodged, the familiar
as contingency. Perseverance
led me to this dwarf
island, my one compass the albatross's
steady unbroken flight. The air
is thin and simple, and brethren
to my bones. Voices do not call
through the mist, no hands
gather me. At night
I whisper. The dark
does not reply.

*

Exhausted, exhumed,
feet aching for the certainty
of an earth, home is the body
I leave from, home is a past
where mothers slather mayonnaise
on ham sandwiches and we
are assured. Every day the sun rises
from the spires of mountain peaks,
and every day the tides roll up the coast
to uproot the rootless and small.
I walk beaches collecting seashells
and water-worn glass, glance lizards
scurrying among dead, decaying growth.
It is always warm.

*

My dreams are prophecy
from myself to myself, and my legs
often do not respond. When into
your house I step, I embrace the offerings.
When entering my abode,
please set aside the resolve.

*

Pardon Me

I woke late and stood on the porch.

Mrs Fudjinski, bent over in her garden, snipped
Sprigs of thyme and basil. Behind her

A cardinal lit on a maple, a shudder
Among the green, through which, out in the bay,

White sails floated against a patch of blue.
Then a breeze stirred the hedgerow,

And turning, I noticed a hummingbird
And yellow jackets flecked thick with

Pollen. I wanted to share this moment
But what the moment was I could not say.

And then it slipped away.

"The Stained Glass . . . Yet Waiting to Be Installed"[2]

Robin's Island stands stately and pristine,
barely touched by human design, just as
it might have through morning mist to Corchaugs
knee deep in tidal silt, digging with feet
for clam. To them, it was Anchannok, "place
thick with trees." Now the island is symbol
and galvanizes a disparate group
of people who battle to preserve it
as memorial to development
everywhere rampant. For those who anchor
off its thin spit the island offers on
listless summer afternoons a harbor
for beers and barbeque. For most, however,
the island is simply there, constant,
inconsequential, like a rock is there,
like a moon is always there though sometimes
veiled in darkness into which a woman
steps. Tonight an unease she cannot name,
something mercurial in the flesh pulls
her from sleep to stand on a wooden deck,
a Spirit in hand. All around autumn
settles in, the air flush with wood smoke and
chill. In the distance geese clamor, a car
motors down New Suffolk Road and thins
into silence, its hush echoing in
the hollow of her ears, disturbing the
already disturbed for nothing here is calm
except the flat waters lipping the shore
where she glances the girl who summered here,

thrashing wildly, arms and legs akimbo.
Here in the shoals of the Great Peconic
Bay she learned to swim, but only out there
beyond the lee of Robin's Island in
water over her head did her fear of
the deep below give way; she let go
and was carried by the water's buoyant
embrace. Her father once carried her on
his shoulders. They would scour the shoreline
for translucent sea glass, blues ones the prize.
She hears him now. *Relax . . . let go, let go*
as she leans on the railing, her eyes fixed on
the darkness stretched before her, against which
is silhouetted the greater darkness
of Robin's Island, stately and pristine,
barely touched. *Relax, let go.* But nothing
happens, nothing ever does anymore,
life a routine. She takes one last drag, snubs
the butt, then turns to ready for sleep where
she dreams a dream in which she floats in
a vast immeasurable unbounded blue.

A Thought Problem

In the *Bhagavad Gita*, as a means toward understanding, a simile
Is employed: "as fire by smoke, as a mirror by dust, as a newborn

By its covering, all is clouded by desire," and of desire Lacan writes
That it is generated through a fundamental lack around which Being

Wraps itself, hoping to be whole again, the paradox being
That to be one is to verge on the zero where the self dissipates

Into the oceanic, a rarity, perhaps, except in death, and of death we die
A little, so say the 17th century French *philosophes*, with each orgasm,

The I given over to an ecstatic disassembling where the light fades
And consciousness elides as in sleep such that when I awaken

To an afternoon melting in the lush courtyard greens
And a random music seeping through the din of faraway traffic,

I shudder at the touch of my lover tucked into my side
Like a question mark, and turn away, afraid of the fire.

Perhaps

On the Battery City Promenade
An elderly woman and her still
Attentive daughter lean over the rail,
Exclaiming. A mother hurries a gaggle
Of adolescents into posing for
A snapshot. A bicyclist brakes, then straddles
The bike, his eyes widening. Strollers slow
Their pace. All are joined to a sun flaming
The westward facing facades and under-
Side of clouds with a brilliance that rivets
Attention. And as soon, the flickering's gone.
The woman gathers her daughter, the Polaroid
Wheezes, Sunday blurring to dusk so deftly
No one notices the ashes everywhere falling.

Across

It was the beat of the pauses between
The stirring of wind in the green canopy,

Bird screeches, the scurry across dead
Leaves that startled us into our surroundings.

We became aware of the chill
And lengthening shadows—the idea of home upon

Us, the observers, who look, who
Do not do nor achieve, honing

The craft of contemplation—deliberate,
Reflexive, slow—one step, the next, one

After another, and the fact of our looking
Out from in, seeing.

We stopped on an outcrop, eyes
Grazing a red-tailed hawk

Standing sentinel against
A background of trees mottled

Grey and a larger effusive grey on which
The spectacle of sunset played,

Where we took wing and scissored the sky
For prey, in our eye a band of trekkers below,

Reminded once again of the compact
Between the seer and the seen.

The Annunciation

I

Halved by the horizon and boot black among reed and tall grass
In sway and rustle, a woman
                              The light feathered in her hair,
Who wore not the emblems of our city.
The look of one who had traveled much and returned with less.

    I've tasted good fruit and suffered uneven lashes. I've loved women and man and
    forgiven my desires. If I could speak I would sing of flora and proffer tools to discard.
    On this journey, the finite heave of the receding.

She paused for the wind; a foul smell grazed my cheek.

    Undo yourself until you do nothing. I've sought the bright side of one and listened
    to the signs, found glittering relics of commerce and generation, day upon day.

    Go to where you are tribute and tributary. Go to the hosanna from whence you came.

On the sloped bank of a tamed river come across.
At the changing between sunset and dark.
People hurrying under a moonless night. Much talk,
Much noise, airwaves jammed and guttered.
Here was solemn and a temperate breeze. Here a woman

With bits of grass and grey in her beak.

II

Define the absence bruised into words
or the pellet impacted in the brain.

Step again inside my room
and divine the toiletries.

I've got plenty
and you can have it.

I've the dull rapture of the idiot,
coming closer to nowhere fast.

III

I, too, Mr Hass, and not
on the wings of a swan
verging on river mist
but the gull, hundreds of them,
stitching the sky in wide
broken spirals, pulling me inward
little by little, dissolving
the substantial until raised high
and dissolute. The last I saw was
my body a speck on the beach
where others were huddled coupled
and in groups contrary to
the January sea. But that was as far
as I went when I was given over.

IV

They come from Tokyo
COD, from Costa Rica
virtual free, from dreams in the
hoarfrost of March and an
afternoon's relief they come.

They come nonstop
without rest or victual,
sudden in strangers,
clamoring and
cackling, dizzy
with contradiction.

They come offering
transition. They come
giddy with fever, they
eager to rehearse their speech.
Call they angels, call they muses,
in droves they come
and place a rune in my ear

to repair in this,
oh frankincense, oh myrrh.

V

Sunday, St Lucia's bell, the dying and their close ones on knees praying.

Death awaits us all.

Three floors up in a room bordering a garden, it waits us.

It sits keen scouring its domain, the contusion of things brilliant in their evanescing.

Soon leaves fall and bodies ache, soon winter then spring and bodies ache.

It suffers not.

The Copake General store is closed and people hike Bash Bish Falls.

A bomb detonates in Tenerif and a door no longer creaks.

And half a world away a woman near a foot bridge waits.

And half a world away a woman is departing, strangers linked in a world away.

VI

>Where is the edge of wind?
>Bow and attend.
>In the whorl of an echo.
>
>Where the edge of speech?
>In the varnish of friction.
>The calligraphy of dunes.
>
>And in the middle of the night
>The brief desert bloom
>Kissed with dew.

VII.

a farrago of fractal menageries and cacophonous teachings.

VIII.

There were days they visited
without warning. I woke dry mouthed
tasting sleep, hair tangled
in hair, hips saddled
to mine. And them too, hovering,
cow-like in the humidity,
moving without displacement—
daemonic, possessed, and stupid
with pleasure. And when you blinked
awake, they quickened into your irises,
a confetti of iridescence
coalescing into my reflection
bent over to welcome
your arrival.

IX.

In the *Bhagavad Gita*, it is written that in the final faring forward
of wayward travelers, in the moment of leaving, the moment

to which you have already been delivered, if one fixes the internal gaze fast to
Krishna, all quiets. Hear not the clunk and clangor of deliberation. Hear

in the distance closing quick in the whirring window instantaneous, the light
blistering to a blur, Them luminaries, dumbly providential and buzzing:

"May you be most awake when you pass."

Breath

"Why are there beings . . . rather than nothing," Heidegger writes, arriving from a future
Already happened to sit before a window overlooking the grey flat pavers of Freiburg, to which

Our physics answers, at least for this universe, because the beginning conditions were just so
Rigorously right that in the turbulent ecstasy of the initial expansion ripples in the plasma

Nucleated & matter and mass evolved so in what we experience as time a solar system
Emerges, our earth far enough from the sun not to sizzle and burn & close enough

Not to freeze, a matter of infinitesimal degrees, where a conjunction of elemental
Molecules joined into life, but as for beginnings, from where comes It, the primal

Beginning, the Ur of all beginnings, & what lies beyond where the universe
Turns on itself, which for humans in their being Socrates in language plain & simple

Commands his pupils to "Know thyself," that is look inward, for "an unexamined life
Is a life not worth living," a dictum Emerson, centuries later in rugged American individualism,

Echoes where a child on the banks of the Sheepscot watches the river
Flow, & I find myself adrift on a blustery Saturday waiting a winter storm, alone,

My vision clotted with a row of evergreens, a few houses & a country lane that Aristotle
Suggests constitute me when he claims the soul is, when paraphrased,

"Identical with the objects of our experience," to mean, I am the flurry dusting the tree, &
The pileated woodpecker hammering for grub in a dead oak is the scratch in my ear,

The tingling in my eye, a radical link intimated by Husserl, so when tonight, my lost
Lover and oracular wife, no longer here fully fleshed in vainglorious and wrinkled

Complementarity, let us mingle in our desiccated skins, let interdependence ring,
For the world is known only in being it, a saying from the Upanishads, such that

In tasting the pine-sour lining the twin berms of your labia, bees waggle, & in cupping
The gravity and auroras of your breasts, the brown bear in hibernation turns over,

A Higgs Boson is traced, & when together we come, if ever, we dissolve, the God inside
Released, this from the Gospels, into the infinite everywhere present, to become no more.

The Holy Ghost

There we always were, in always again, enjambed helter skelter on a Sealy
Posturepedic neither could leave. Outside cranes pounded the earth, & dead

Leaves clung to skeletal trees, the air fragrant & crackling.
Money accrued in heaps. Crib deaths mounted. Technology & prayer

Flourished. Little of that mattered where we nestled in the season
Of cuddle & craving, & grew thin, past sadness & anger, sliding in

And out of stillness that was our succor. And hints of the everyday rose brighter
And hotter outside our open portal. We marveled the many lights

Blink off & on, on & off, the stretch of fire furrowed in the night
Sky. Then our hair fell out, from leg, ear & head—pubic fuzz, downy arm,

Stubbled beard—& of the strands long & scratchy we made a nest
For the doves camped outside our windowsill. Next were our teeth,

Then our bodies branching into flame, soon to join the blue black
Archipelago of stars, quantum phantoms in the undivided dark.

Bridge

Sentiment for an Old Notion

Some things are better left unsaid.
Rousseau noticed it in the Nambikwara
in their adamant refusal to appoint
proper names, and there is the superstition
of birthday wishes, that if one desires the wish
fulfilled, one keeps it a secret.
And always those who try to egg it out, the brats
and the envious ones. Rousseau
made children his accomplice, too, by playing
one child against another and through innuendo,
uncovered their names. The children were punished.
He departed unscathed, the true culprit, an intruder.
I knew a woman who one night after lovemaking
told me her story of anorexia, how
she had wanted to die because everything
was named and fixed in such a web
that there "wasn't a fresh corner to breathe in." Death
seemed the fitting excision. I asked her
why she didn't and she one autumn mid
night stood on a bridge poised to
jump. The moon was notched in the valley, mist
rose off the river, and there was the turbulence
of white water reverberating below.
In her periphery, hillsides massed in darkness
and she heard in her ears the faint echo
of birds far downstream. It was the moment
she didn't leap because amidst this presence
she was overtaken by a breathtaking beauty. That
was how she phrased it, "breathtaking." She did not recall

in her mind that the river was the river Reuss
and the bridge the main link between Zurich and Berne,
that beech and Norwegian spruce grew there and that
those birds were brown speckled mallards
in migration and she wanted to say more but stopped
because she was going to say something about love.

Back

A Short Compilation of the History and Uses of Sage

In an effort to discover
& categorize birds "heretofore"
unclassified by European precepts

& for fame,
le Valliant in South Africa
& this his last return.

Inflamed with fever, unable
to swallow but a few drops
of water, he, for Cape Town,

crosses the Kaussi Mountains.
Among the canon shot & cured
meats, the provisions bartered

for information and food, there
is nothing appointed for pain except
muskets. He diagnoses it as quinsy

& almost suffocates. Hottentots
apply hot poultices of boiling cow's milk
& sing. Nothing.

Half moon to full, he writes,
"long, laborious and dangerous
journeys, for what & my collections."

On the eighth day, an elder
from Lesser Numaqua with skin
brighter than coal offers this:

hot compresses of mud
to the throat & a broth
that when gargled tastes

sweet & strident
& rises with "an agreeable smell."
Three days of constant attention

& on the fourth he is
convalescing & commanding.
The remedy:

"Nothing in the country was more common;
it grew all around the camp
and was to be met with in every direction."

        *

Sage sipped as tea
in a candle's halo
soothes the nerves.

She says she says relax—
your butt muscles are too
tight. And when you first enter,

move more slowly. I
want to feel you so we move
together, not as separate wills

She says she says, tea,
two heaping teaspoons, sun cured,
steep five minutes.

Use, however, only the leaves,
not the root, bitter
Latin

from salvare, to be in high health,
not to be confused with sapare,
a different seed signifying the wise,

which in our English married
the same bride. Homonyms.
Peculiar how a plentiful bush

written of by Pliny was
grafted to a quality not so readily
abundant. There are no accidents.

Taken as drink, daily,
in small doses, the plant
dredges from the backwash

of the forgotten,
memory and memory gathers with age
as does experience, no?

I have heard that wisdom
is no more than a fool's experiences
contemplated—once burned

twice learned—and that a fool
is marked
by his words. I can see

the anonymous ones, cross-
legged, sedentary, under the oleander
with a cow-like dumbness

printed in their devout
unmentionable faces,
a ceramic bowl set in front

to which lips curl round
in one graceful swoop.
Our lovemaking heightens.

She says I'm so touchable
after we love, don't
say anything, she says she says . . .

                    *

Thunder here means longer days,
an arousal from winter's rigidity.
Those spartan landscapes

rife with brooding
now point toward apical meristems
& green thoughts in a green shade,

a lightening, for example.
Once the word was despair
& I wedged it among the inflexible

pattern of dailiness
& in the woman I was with
unlike dogwood

which is seasonal
with perfect flowers, bracts
brown tipped. Here

under dampened branches, the air
livens with hints
of warmth & blossomings of color,

azaleas bright clustered
& scarcely fragrant to the diminutive
nose hurrying

on its way to the market
to purchase dinner set
for one, perhaps two, maybe three.
                    *

Sage I have tasted—
a balmy, mid-winter day,
a deserted beach

& the mewing of gulls
listing toward silence. I remember
remembering.

The sun was straight up, still
tide. The vastness. When back among
things I could name like the boardwalk

flared purple with dusk
& dusk touched by a frothy sea,
my lips were chapped

& gulls huddled tight,
their solemn unmoving heads
leaning leeward into the wind,

high water, a circle ringing
a moon feral & dominant. Five
hours & no accounting for the time.

Vastness. That night, Peter,
afraid for my welfare, kept
me company with his care

& once again with trust
lodged numinously in a world,
we spoke the other language,

a gaze,
a touch,
tears.
                    *

In China, in 1578, Li Shih-chen
after 26 years trodding
countrysides includes sage,

salvia japonica,
in his medical treatise
Pen Ts'ao. He names it

Shu-wei ts'ao
because of its peculiar flower spikes
& calls it

Wu-ta'ao when used by women
to dye black their flaxen hair.
When by a riverbank, you kick

back to watch clouds
sidle overhead, look to your right—
a thicket combed in muddy grounds

where among the many
stalks are a group, weedy
& fuzzy leafed, call it

Shu-ch'ing because
it is found near water.
He prescribes "the white flowered kind

is good for colorless discharges
& the red flowered for red
discharges." How simple!

Mash the plant
with other herbs & you have
a treatment

for goiter & flux,
a clinical term for
"too much shitting."

& as a tea, "relief
from the pains & aches"
of dropsy, & much safer than aspirin.
                    *

Farmers & mystic acolytes
planted the seed
in sandy soil come March or early

April when the bitten air
yielded to warming currents.
By May, buds.

In times of drought
& uncertainty they looked
for signs, they besieged

the world for answers—
leaves robust or browning
at the edges, curling under;

stem firm or
sagging, fortune's
signature to be deciphered.

Today is a ripe
avocado
& solitude. It is

a single speed beach cruiser
leaning against a hedge and bees
drunk on yellow flowers.

Today I know destiny
like the Greeks knew fusion,
and the not knowing is good.

                    *

That sage is a bush,
that the word sage follows,
but which sage,

sage, benevolent
& wise, or sage,
a dicotyledon

with slender stalks, ovary
superior, stamens less
in number than corolla lobes.

Or more precise, leaves
basal or on the stem, toothed
or smooth, annual or perennial,

calyx tubular or campanulate,
in Florida or the Cote du Azur
growing in open fields.

Or now in my tea. Or as
script & concept,
sage, genus

verbancea, officialis
& sapien, two legged with opposite
thumbs & highly developed

frontal cortex. I knew
an old woman who wore
intricately patterned kimonos

and wooden sandals. She tended
a garden. In it, plants, but not
the ornamental sort.

She would pick their leaves. Mother
warned me away. Still I would sneak by
to hear her stories

of samsara, of bathing
under tanned skies, how she settled
in Kyoto prefecture, one husband, one death.

I came to her curious.
I came to her with poison ivy.
Two days later it subsided,

I came hoarse with sore throat.
This she concocted: one drachm cayenne,
water & an ounce of, you

guessed it, sage. She died before I left
Japan, her garden cramped
with weeds & crows pecking away

at whatever remained.
The practice,
the curiosity.
                    *

She said: I will come, come
I will. Only asters
& goldenrods break the wind,

bullfrogs in choral groan.
By the footbridge I listened.
Now she writes:

No!
A low fire warms
the one room cabin. Sleep

has already taken me
when the door, unlatched,
slams shut.
                    *

Twilight entwined
in the bramble of the prickly,
a blazing afternoon

walking to Matala
to meet no one I know,
the back way, through parched

countryside treacherous
with caves and loose ground.
I angled a goat

path cut
into rock & overrun
with thistle and thorn until

among tourists and strangers.
At the local cantina
before a makeshift wood table

I order a small glass
of retsina, the porous
earth come up

in the local green
grape, bitter
yet quenching & cheap.

Such good memories linger
days the heat is strong,
shade so very vital.

Sunday

I want to think it enough
that an elderly couple groomed
for an afternoon stroll on a day
in April unexpectedly warm and bright
sits on a bench overlooking the Hudson
and together scans the gloaming
over New Jersey, saying little, when
the man suddenly stands and shuffles
to her side to shield her
from a northwesterly blowing
across her shoulder.

Endnotes

1. The poem is intended to be read in a sing-songy lilt like that of a parent reading a bedtime story to a child.

2. The poem's title is a quote from a book on Robins Island and refers to the house that Mr Lane, in the early 1800s, was building for his wife. She fell to pneumonia during its construction and died. Mr Lane, heartbroken, abandoned its completion.

Afterword

This book is culled from the many poems written over my seventy years of living. Early in my adult life I wanted to make a career of poetry. Life, however, intervened, and other paths emerged, which when considered revealed a theme, or so I think from the vantage of now. Still, the poems existed. Though they had spawned from my imagination, they deserved a chance to be regarded on their own. Thus, the book.

There are many, many people I am indebted to, people who influenced me deeply and people who influenced me faintly yet nonetheless left a trace. I want to acknowledge all, but memory is capricious, and while faces appear, names do not, and then there are the memories weathered by age and dormancy into omission. I do not want to offend so take the chicken shit way out and list no one, hoping if by chance this book you come across, you know who you are, know that our lives touched and like bubbles in a stream joined together, however long and short a time it was, however joyous or hurtful our interactions were, and all the shadings in between. Forgive me this dishonor, for I know deep down, we want to be acknowledged and recognized.

But, most ironically, as evidenced by the Supreme Court ruling that corporations indeed hold rights like those of individuals—can you believe that—I want to thank the institutions that supported me in this endeavor. First there is the College of William and Mary where I discovered poetry. Then the Peace Corps which afforded time, between the seasonal work, to deepen my reading and knowledge of poetry. Then a year of poetry workshops in NYC at the School of General Studies at Columbia University, the 92nd Street Y, and a private one held in Westbeth Artists Housing. That year was followed by two years at the MFA Writing Program at Columbia University, where I honed the craft of writing, led by the gifted poets teaching there and my peers in the program. There were residencies at the Karolyi Foundation in Vence, France, and The Virginia Center for the Creative Arts in Sweet Briar, Virginia, and an offer from The McDowell Foundation in Peterborough, New Hampshire that fostered me. I thank too the Center for Modern Psychoanalytic Studies and the Center for Group Studies, where I studied psychoanalysis and encountered my current analysts, and the Center for Medicine Work in Wyndmoor, Pennsylvania where I am now in training. Lastly, though not least, are the journals, others than those listed in the front matter, where poems not in this book were originally published: *Phoebe, Columbia: A Magazine of Poetry and Prose, New Guardian Literary Review, The Ocotiillo Review, The Alaska Quarterly Review, Hayden's Ferry Review, Blue Mountain Review, Harbinger Asylum, Poeming Pie-gon*, and *Think: A Journal of Fiction, Poetry, and Essays.*

I also honor the plant medicines, which birthed this destiny from my once wayward soul . . .

And the one name I am going to utter, my love interest and partner, Judith Aley. Thank you for being.

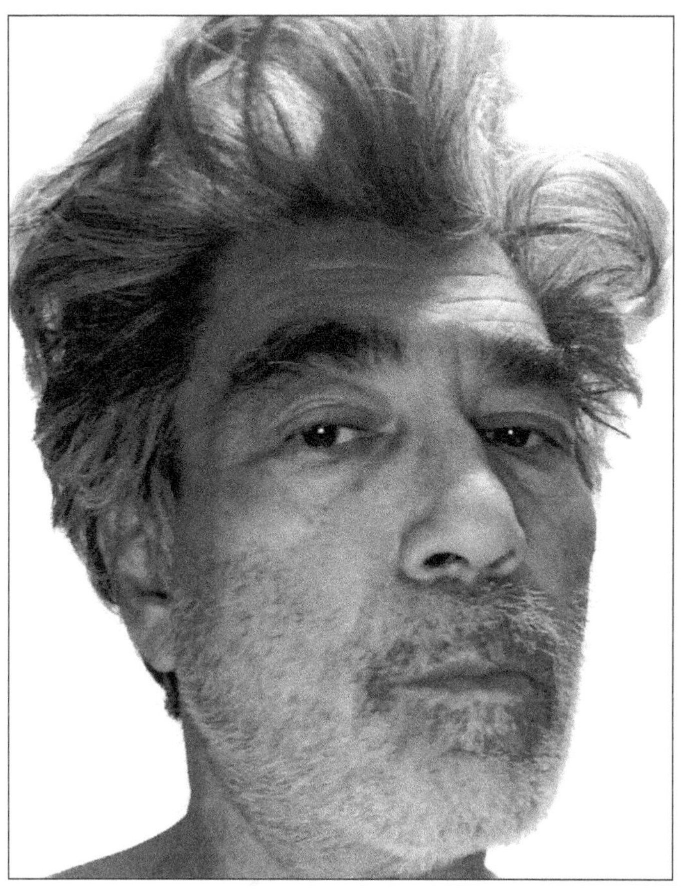

Ronald Okuaki Lieber is now a proud grandfather to Jackson Okuaki Sherwood
and looks forward to the lineage continuing. www.ronaldokuakilieber.com